EMPLOYEE ENGAGEMENT

EMPLOYEE ENGAGEMENT

WHAT THE HOSPITALITY INDUSTRY IS MISSING

RANDY STARR
chief engagement officer
rjs data group

DEDICATION

This book is dedicated to my wife, Johnetta. She is the inspiration of my life. She has supported every ridiculous thing I have done over the last 23-plus years. She's the best wife in the world!

FORWARD

This book was written after about 12 years of reviewing engagement surveys from businesses in the hospitality industry. Being the CEO of rjs data group has given me deep insight into how organizations treat their employees. Before establishing rjs data group, I worked in hotels for close to 20 years. I started my career as a front desk clerk, an hourly paid employee. Working my way up the ladder, I learned that employees are the key to running a successful operation.

ACKNOWLEDGMENTS

I wish to acknowledge my family for being so
supportive; Dale Carnegie Training; Gallup; my
wonderful LinkedIn colleagues; Don Butto, who
created the cover; and my editor Douglas Glen Clark

CONTENTS

1 WHAT IS ENGAGEMENT?

I remember when I first heard how J. Willard Marriott built his hotel empire. "You've got to make your employees happy," he said. "If the employees are happy, they are going to make the customers happy." I am pretty sure he knew what he was doing, given that he took a root beer stand to what some consider the number one hotel business in the world. He did that by taking care of his employees. His statement alone implies that he was genuinely concerned for his employees. I remember meeting and working with Marriott employees who had worked for the company for very long periods of time. Some had met Mr. Marriott, some had worked for him personally, and none ever had a negative comment. They liked him—a lot!

> "You've got to make your employees happy. If the employees are happy, they are going to make the customers happy." – J. Willard Marriott

They had respect for him and would do anything to make him proud. They were engaged. When he was creating the culture for his company, he paid a lot of attention to his hourly employees. When they were sick, he would visit them; when they got into trouble, he would help them get out of it. He thus created a loyal family. When I was growing up, a worker who showed that type of loyalty was called a "company man" because he would do whatever he could to help the company. Today we call that type of worker a highly engaged employee.

What is Your Definition?

This is where the critical thinking begins: What is engagement? You can use the dictionary definition, a promise or pledge, or you can choose your own. Being somewhat active on LinkedIn, I found it quite interesting when a member of the Employee Engagement group posed the question, "In one word can you tell what engagement means to you?" This online conversation continues to produce hundreds of answers. That should shed a little light on the problem: If hundreds of professional human resources managers can't agree on a definition how can they possibly promote engagement or resolve their issues? Or could it be that engagement is a broad term that embraces varied definitions and that the issues are not being resolved because we are addressing them only with our narrow definitions?

In my attempt to help you and your organization move beyond your current level of engagement and create better work environments, I am going to keep this book as simple as possible. I hope you will not need to pull out old textbooks to brush up on theories and remind yourself how some research company explains these theories and their relationships with the inner workings of our psyches. I am not going to attempt to impress you with my vast vocabulary, nor will I try to impress you by making things complex and complicated, I promise.

Defining the problem of engagement is not as easy as it may seem. I start to define engagement in the workplace as environment, or at least the perceived environment of the employee. "Perceived" is a key word, and here is where it starts to get a bit confusing. My perception is my reality, and your perception is your reality. But at times our perceptions may differ, even if we are in the same environment. Example: Have you ever had a co-worker who had issues with a supervisor about which you did not agree? Both of you are in the same environment but have different perceptions. I can't tell you how many times I have read comments from a group of employees who have the same supervisor, and some of them love the supervisor and the others have multiple issues with him or her. Why? Is it because the supervisor treats some better than others? Yes, at least in their perception.

> My perception is my reality, and your perception is your reality.

This is a double-edged sword. Supervisors are human, and they react to employees differently based on their perceptions. So they gradually make good relationships better and poor relationships worse if nothing is done to make changes.

It is important to point out that there are three distinct areas of engagement in the eyes of the employees, as was determined by Dale Carnegie Training.

- *Relationship with their immediate supervisor*
- *Belief in senior leadership*
- *Pride in working for the company*

My research tends to support this finding. Employees spend most of their time working with or around their immediate supervisors. Theirs is a key relationship for engagement. This should make you rethink the way you select your supervisors, starting now. How many times have we promoted hourly employees to supervisory positions because they were excellent at their jobs? For some reason, we tend to think that an awesome housekeeper will make an awesome housekeeping supervisor; some do, but not all. Employees get to know their supervisors better than they know other management members, so the attitude and behavior of the supervisor is under constant scrutiny. A supervisor who is not walking the walk is actually disengaging employees.

Then comes senior leadership. Employees must believe that the senior leaders are competent and making decisions that benefit the business. Employees need to receive communication from senior leaders about the business; they want to hear the goals, challenges and accomplishments. They want to know what is going on.

Pride in the company is also important. Employees need to feel respect from the organization; they need to believe that like they are being heard and not treated as just numbers on a payroll program somewhere at the corporate office.

Looking at Differences

We have seen that defining engagement is partly a function of recognizing the diverse definitions we hold in our heads and complicated by our individual perceptions of our environments. We can't standardize the perceptions of our employees because they come from different backgrounds with different beliefs, different feelings and different thought processes. It appears, therefore, that engagement has strong links with relationships. In the example above, the supervisors more than likely have better relationships with the workers who view them in a positive light. Relationships are probably strained or nonexistent with workers who view their supervisors negatively.

We are not getting into rocket science here, but relationships can be just as difficult. The workplace is full of relationships, and the one who masters those wins. Take average workers in America and the number of relationships they have at work with co-workers, supervisors and management in their own departments. Add any relationships they may have in other departments and relationships with corporate support teams, and it starts to become obvious that relationships have an overwhelming effect on engagement. Let's face it, if you enjoy the people you work with and for, you can accomplish a lot more.

2 THE RESEARCH

It is important to understand where my conclusions and views come from. I did not just pull them out of the air. After almost 20 years of working in the hotel business, I started rjs data group to provide cost-effective, efficient and value-rich engagement survey solutions to the hospitality industry, an alternative to the efforts of large data collection companies. We developed our systems based on feedback from human resources managers in the industry; we attended several major conferences with no product to promote, just questions for the end users. Once this process was complete, we developed the systems and went to work. Over the last dozen years, we have surveyed millions of employees in hotels, restaurants, casinos, healthcare facilities and corporate offices. This diversified respondent pool comes from the United States, Canada, Mexico and some countries in South America. These respondents speak many languages, but they have much in common.

Opossums in the Kitchen

Many of the respondents share comments, usually in a text box or freehand question at the end of the survey. I remember when our first survey results started coming in from hotels across the U.S. At that time, the surveys were done on paper and data entry employees were responsible for entering the answers and comments. One of the employees read a comment out loud, "Somebody has to do something about all these opossums in the kitchen," and of course the room burst into laughter. After that, I started reading the comments, but with no particular purpose. Some were short, some were voluminous. They ranged from humorous to alarming. I also started reading the comments that had been translated from foreign languages back into English, before they were added to reports. By now, I have read hundreds of thousands of employee comments. They are very telling, and I soon started noticing trends and commonalities.

> "Somebody has to do something about all these opossums in the kitchen."

I started comparing findings from the comments and to the actual questionnaire results. The comments backed up and validated the scores, and in most cases they went deeper.

I continue to read comments to this day, and I've noticed another interesting pattern: Most of the comments can be placed in one of five general categories. These categories are the areas that are overlooked at many countries across the nation and in all labor- intensive operations.

The areas that we as leaders in operations need to improve:

Communication   **Training**

Respect

Recognition   **Fairness**

The Five Cornerstones

These five basic areas are the cornerstones for developing an engaged employee. The concept seems pretty simple, and it is. Sometimes, however, simple is not easy. These precepts are the basics in creating an environment conducive to engagement. If we communicate effectively and frequently, train our employees to the best of our ability, show respect, give recognition and treat workers fairly, we will be on the road to developing an engaged employee.

Think about your current situation. Are your supervisors and managers employing these cornerstones consistently? Do you believe that your immediate supervisor or the person to whom you report is consistently employing these cornerstones with you? If not, you can change the culture within your organization I will discuss how to make culture shifts and changes in a subsequent chapter of this book.

Although these areas are woven tightly together, I believe it is important to address them individually, drawing from personal experience and showing examples of comments and feelings from surveyed employees. As we go through this process, please remember this is simple, just basic common sense.

3 COMMUNICATION

Were you as shocked as I was when you saw that communication is an issue? We live in the age of communication and the means by which we communicate—email, cellphones, text messages, Facebook, Twitter, FaceTime, Snapchat—have grown exponentially and will surely continue to do so. Ways to communicate are more accessible now than ever, with cellphones and easily portable laptops, tablets and cameras.

So why do organizations fail miserably when it comes to communicating with their employees? I don't believe the cause is an innate inability to communicate. Could it be that the confusion is the result of the many and varied methods of communication available? Possibly, but I doubt it. I think the culprit is a combination of factors, one of which is that an organization may be stuck in a rut when it comes to communication.

Many have been communicating with their employees in a certain way for years and can't or won't change. They deem the method to be effective and think employees should simply conform. I have seen printed memos pinned or taped to walls in break rooms, the method some managers have chosen to convey rather important information to their employees. I am not saying this is ineffective, but I would point out that the memo was probably created on a computer that had the email addresses of all the employees. Wouldn't it have been more effective to send an email? And what if the same computer has all the employees' cellphone numbers as well, allowing for a quick and effective text message? This is just one example of methods that may or may not be effective for your organization.

REI Inc., a manufacturer of outdoor gear and apparel, makes use of modern technology with what it calls its online company campfire, which allows employees and executives to share thoughts and discuss issues in a very intimate fashion.

SAP, a world leader in business software, has a culture of collaboration, which means that communication is vital to its success. One of its main focuses is called listening loudly, because there is a difference between listening and hearing.

Your Communication Skills

You should evaluate your personal communication. Is it effective? Are you communicating frequently? Do you ever procrastinate when it comes to communication?

Let's look at effective communication first. The best way to communicate effectively is to maintain simple language and a simple message. You are effective when everyone who receives your message understands it completely. In most circumstances, you should get to the point. Don't beat around the bush and try to warm up the recipients by giving them unwanted information. Your communications should be direct and respectful at all times. rjs data group has a company philosophy of keeping it simple, keeping communication on a sixth-grade level. Obviously there are many components to rjs data group that are extremely technical and require some technical communication, but that communication is limited to the geeks. Please take no offense at the term, which my good friend and business partner chose to call that department. He is our CGO—chief geek officer—and we think it's funny. The CEO in my title stands for chief engagement officer. I should point out that the CGO and I have a unique relationship; friends and business partners for more than a dozen years—all on a handshake. I believe that we both use the five pillars quite well.

Inevitably you will have some communication that is not simple and needs to be extremely technical. In such cases, just remember the audience. Other than those rare occasions, keep it simple. When you do that, everyone understands more quickly. Your employees will grasp the meaning without having to decipher your language and figure out your intent.

I Am Smarter Than You

I used to have a boss who thought he had climbed the ladder because of his superior control of the English language and his huge intellect. I really liked the guy, but half of his emails were trashed immediately and the other half were skimmed and then trashed. They were ridiculous; I seriously needed a thesaurus to get through a paragraph. I wasted so much time trying to understand his communication that it was funny. He wanted to impress upon all his vast knowledge and vocabulary, but in reality, no one cared and most thought he was weird. Let your ability in getting things done properly the first time be what impresses others about you.

> Half of his emails were trashed and the other half were skimmed and then trashed.

How frequently do you communicate? Probably not often enough. The best communication is face to face or face to faces. Get out of your office and manage by walking around, a vital concept to which I will return later in this book). The people doing the work know what can make their jobs or tasks easier; see if they will tell you. They also know what is being done incorrectly, so get off your butt and go talk to everyone you can. Have impromptu meetings and stand ups, limit them to five minutes tops, ask direct questions and move along.

I have read many comments about the lack of availability of managers. They seem to be in the office all day long or otherwise unavailable. This is not the best way to create a relationship with your staff. You need to be visible, approachable and friendly.

Get to know the people you work with. This type of communication starts to develop relationships, and when you develop relationships, you start to earn respect and trust. This will enable your team to be more productive because, when employees are not worried about how or when communication will happen, they can focus on the tasks at hand. Open, direct and frequent communication is a way to eliminate the minor issues that people get stuck on and that lower productivity. Some describe such minor issues as workplace drama. Eliminating the drama is almost impossible, but dealing with the drama tends to diminish it, and the time it takes from start to end is significantly reduced.

Let Me Tell You How You are Doing—Later

There is another form of communication mentioned quite frequently in comments from employees: performance management. Most organizations have a formal performance management tool, which is supposed to be used annually, when an employee receives a performance evaluation from his or her immediate supervisor or manager.

Having done thousands of these over the course of my career, I have difficulty understanding why most organizations don't do a better job at this key piece of communication. Or rather, I do understand to a degree. We regularly hear that performance evaluations are not conducted on a timely manner.

The process is rather simple and in most cases a fill-in-the-blanks situation, yet management tends to procrastinate. There are several reasons for this, the most prevalent being that most employees do not like negative feedback; therefore most managers don't like it either. Most people try to avoid confrontation, so if the review is going to be negative, they'd rather just put it off, hoping that it will somehow get better. It won't; it will get worse.

That approach applies to negative reviews, but what about the ones for your "A" team? These are going to be positive and uplifting, so why would they also be delayed? Could it be because performance reviews have coincided historically with pay raises?

> If the review is going to be negative, some managers would rather just put it off.

Over the last several years, most organizations have frozen wages or have limited pay increases because of the sluggish economy. At the same time, however, we have often asked our employees to do more work and take on more responsibility for no extra compensation. For this reason, even a good review can be a negative experience. The employee has done a stellar job and gets an excellent review, but he or she gets little to no compensation for efforts and commitment.

Not many managers enjoy going into performance reviews with tremendous employees, telling them how well they have done and then giving them fifty-cent-an-hour raises. Think about that for just a minute: You have asked employees to perform additional duties and they have done so; and you may have even asked them to do the jobs of three people; and you are giving them a raise of $4 a day for these additional responsibilities. Wow! I bet that goes over well. This is why the performance evaluation has become another double-edged sword.

I suggest a few changes for performance evaluations.

We were taught to deliver negative feedback sandwiched with positive, right? That approach is not as effective today as it was 20 years ago, probably because we have used it way too often in the past; and now it could actually work against you.

I believe that performance evaluations should not be restricted to the formal annual review period; they should be part of the daily routine, linked to the business strategy of the organization.

Strategies

I believe it is important to compensate performance, but one must be aware that this system can be flawed it can that pay levels should not be attached to performance evaluations because, in a lot of cases, it create negatives when employees know that their performance is related to their pay; promotions and financial rewards (bonus) can drive or encourage employees to hide or cover up mistakes they make. This process can breeds dishonesty.

I could write an entire book on performance management but will instead leave you with this: Assessments should happen frequently, a minimum of four times a year. Assessment meetings should be more focused on growth than on what was done wrong.

That seems pretty simple, right? You have been communicating since you were born, so now it is time to be just a little more conscious of how, when and why you are communicating. Keep the message simple, so everyone can understand it immediately. When less time is spent deciphering your message, more time can be spent on being productive. Clarity should govern printed notes as well. Sometimes it is best to spell out all the words in a handwritten note; abbreviations seem to be the way of the future, but your first priority is making sure the audience understands the communication.

In summary, to communicate effectively with your employees, get out there and roll up your sleeves. Get to know your team members, and let them get to know you. Be yourself, not the boss. When you don't communicate, you create issues that take time to resolve, and those issues can haunt you for a long time. If you take the time to communicate, everyone benefits.

4 TRAINING

It seems to me that almost every organization has some form of training program. Some offer more depth than others, but every organization I ever worked for had some sort of program to help new employees learn about the company philosophy and history and how to properly perform the tasks they were hired to complete. I don't believe that there is a lack of training processes.

Why Throw Them to the Wolves?

I do believe, however, that good qualities may be missing from some of the processes regularly administered by some managers. New employees are hired to fill a void, a position that may have been vacant too long, so that work needs to be done immediately. This can result in a lack of proper initial training, and newly hired people are thus sometimes thrown to the wolves.

Speeding up training of a new employee is the worst possible decision for all involved. First, it can create a terrible first impression for the employee, who is put in an unnecessary and extremely stressful situation. Remember that a new employee will attempt to do well and make a good first impression, while you are setting the stage for failure. Speedy training also creates a negative for the customer. You are reducing the expected level of service by letting a poorly trained employee have contact with customers.

I will never forget when I learned this the hard way. I was managing a hotel that was financially successful and the turnover was low, but a front desk employee unexpectedly resigned to take a better-paying position in another industry after she finished her education. That left us with a void that needed to be filled immediately, and because we were in a very good labor market, we had many applicants. After a week of interviewing, **we** hired a new front desk employee. I say "we" because I always made interviewing and hiring a committee process. Rarely did I make the decision myself. Instead, **I** let the team that would be working with the new employee make the decision. This person then needed to go through training for at least one week, but probably closer to 10 days. This process required the new employee to spend time in the "classroom" as well as shadowing people from other departments and finally working side by side with a senior person at the desk.

The Phone Call

In the middle of this process, the new employee answered an incoming call from what everyone assumed was a guest or potential guest. Instead, it was a call for me from my regional manager. Answering the phone is a simple thing, right? But if the phone is actually a switchboard and you have not been officially trained in transferring calls, it is pretty easy to make a mistake. That's what the new employee did, transferred my boss to a nonexistent extension that rang and rang and rang. He hung up and called back; the phone was answered by a different employee and transferred to my office successfully. The first question out of his mouth: "Why is it that the first thing we have untrained employees do is answer the phone? Seems like most people calling the hotels are guests or potential guests. Do we really want to give them a bad first impression?" Ouch! Point taken.

> They want to learn different jobs so they can further their careers and help the organization.

When you don't use your training systems, you are creating issues that will take time to overcome. Use the time to train properly, and everyone benefits.

It is amazing to me that so many employees request cross-training. They want to learn different jobs so they can further their careers and help the organization meet its goals. Cross-training is a huge asset to management, so why are we not constantly cross-training? If you have employees who can work in any position or multiple positions, you have your bases covered, so the customer will be well-served. Cross-training may take some time, but everyone will benefit.

5 RESPECT

We have all heard that respect must be earned, right? You get some respect for your position and the fact that you are a human, but the kind of respect that encourages people do things for you is not a given. This type of respect is earned by developing relationships, working side by side with your staff, getting to know them and letting them get to know you. This type of respect, a key element of engagement, will have senior employees telling new employees how much they admire the supervisor, manager or company, calling their employers real people who have their employees' best interests in mind, because it's true. This informal endorsement is worth its weight in gold. It says you know that you can't do all the work yourself and that you know you need others to help you every day. It says you know you need a group of individuals who love to work with you and with everyone else in the group you have developed.

If You Don't...

Some people have a skewed view of respect, one that is a bit dated or even ancient. Respect and fear are opposites, although some people somehow manage to get them mixed up. A true leader does not have to threaten an employee with job loss, fewer hours, additional work or an unfavorable schedule. If you find yourself doing so, and if you wonder why you don't have the respect of your entire team, I've just told you. It's pretty simple stuff: People want to be treated with respect, and you must respect your employees before they will respect you.

I will never forget when I was given the first assignment that put me in charge of an entire housekeeping department. Honestly, it was a bit scary. The department was made up of some rather senior employees who had been working in housekeeping for many years, and they knew how to do their jobs very well. When I was introduced to them, I am pretty sure they could smell the fear on me. I did have one thing going for me, though; I had worked in housekeeping for a week in my training class. These few days in training at a small property in Detroit taught me one thing for sure: I did not want to be a housekeeper. Before that training, I had no idea how nasty people could be in hotel rooms. So, the one thing I had going for me in that assignment was respect. I respected all of these employees tremendously, right off the bat, and they could sense the respect along with the fear. I never asked them to do anything that I was not willing to do or had already done. I worked alongside them from punch-in to punch-out. And I helped them understand elements of the business side of the hotel that they had never been taught before.

> I had no idea how nasty people could be in hotel room.

They had never even heard the term revpar (revenue per available room); they did not understand some of the basic decisions that managers made every day because nobody thought they needed to know. At first, most of them did not even want to know, but I was giving something to them and they were giving something to me. We started to respect one another for the people we were, not for the positions we held or the tasks we performed. As that respect was blossoming, they started to tell me that I did not need to work with them any longer, that they understood my mission. Many managers would have thought, "All right! No more housekeeping for me. I have the respect, so now I am out of here." I stayed, though, and built more respect. I also branched out, however, and started to focus some of my efforts in the front office.

Respect is earned over a period of time when you do the right things in the eyes of the ones you work with, the ones you work for and ones you supervise. Do what you are supposed to do, when you are supposed to and do it to the best of your ability; if you do, you will gain respect all around. The practice of working alongside your staff is one that should never stop. It can certainly be reduced over time, but you don't want to hear from one of your staff members that you used to help all the time. If you hear that, it means that you need to get back in there and strengthen the bond.

6 RECOGNITION

Recognition is interesting; some people are driven solely by their desire for recognition; others not so much. But nearly everyone loves some recognition. It comes in all shapes and sizes, formal and informal. Sometimes recognition is private; sometimes it is public, accompanied by huge fanfare. Regardless of the type, recognition for achievement always makes people feel good when their accomplishments are recognized.

Let's think about a form of recognition that is used in a lot of workplaces, the infamous employee of the month award. I am guilty of using this worn out, pathetic and ridiculous sham of a recognition program. Can you tell I am not a fan?

If you are using this type of program in your organization, stop doing so when you get to work tomorrow. This program works well for about three months, then causes more harm than good. Using this approach because you always have done so is horrible. Get creative if you feel you need a formal program. You may be giving away annual awards for certain accomplishments—who sold the most, which unit made the most money, which unit had the best guest scores—so you give an award to the head of that unit, perhaps the general manager.

In my hotel career, I was honored to win many such awards, some of which even came with checks. I still struggle with that type of recognition; I understand that the general manager is the person responsible for getting things done. At the same time, I recognize that there is a large team of people who do the work but who are not getting any recognition.

I think this type of program should dig a bit deeper and reward and recognize the entire staff. If it was a team effort, it should be a team reward.

Thank You So Much!

It's clear that I am not a huge fan of formal recognition programs. Sometimes they may work just fine, but overall I do not think they are an effective long-term vehicle for recognizing employees. Why not recognize employees who have just accomplishing something, like completing a hard day's work? How about recognizing the employee who just went above and beyond to satisfy a customer or exceed their expectations?

> Give your employees the recognition now, and they will immediately want to do a good job again.

The reason you recognize someone for doing something good is so he or she will do it again, right? I am sure there is a theory that could explain this in about 45 pages, but it is simple. When your boss congratulates you for doing a good job on a project,

I'll bet you will be eager to volunteer for the next project, because you want more recognition. So without trying to analyze the motivation, let's just go with the fact that you like the recognition and want more. So why wouldn't you, as a manager, recognize good performance immediately instead of waiting until the end of the month or year? Give your employees the recognition now, and they will immediately want to do a good job again. That just seems logical to me.

We hear time after time that employees believe that they are overworked and underappreciated. This means that as a whole, we are not telling our employees how much we value their efforts. This is a very easy fix: Step up and tell them thank you. Thanks for your efforts today. But be careful: If you have not been doing this, you are going to have to ease into it or your employees   will think you are trying to butter them up for something.

There is an art to thanking someone. Your gratitude should be expressed for something specific. For instance, if a housekeeper works late to get rooms ready for a group of arriving guests, I would identify the extra effort and point out the benefit to the company, in this case that the guests were able to check in with no issues. You many also want to make the thank-you personal, but you can do this only if you know your staff. In the case of the housekeeper, I would mention any sacrifice of time she made to help the company. It's also important to note if the extra effort was appreciated by co-workers and by your own supervisor.

The MBWA Approach

This is something I did every day as a manager because it would allow me to recognize all the employees in front of their peers and at times in front of customers.

Most hotels have a start time and most of the employees have a place where the day's work starts. Whether that's the break room, employee lounge or somewhere in the department, you need to be there when the work day begins. Say your good mornings, give a little information about the day's work, ask if there are any questions and then thank everyone in advance for their efforts. Between start time and lunch, I loved to MBWA (manage by walking around), mainly because I hate sitting down but also because this is when I could connect and create the relationships that benefit everyone.

I believe that managing by walking around is a lost art, which means that many   managers have missed out on a lot of fun at work. I would visit each work station, see if there was anything I could do to assist, ask how the morning was going, say thank you and move to the next work station. At lunch time, I usually made sure I ate with employees, so I could mention anything out of the ordinary from the morning and take the opportunity to publically thank or recognize anyone who had done something worthy. After lunch and before quitting time, I did more managing by walking around, just as I did in the morning. Before leaving for the day, there is often time to wind down, finish paper work, make sure you are ready for the next day, etc. This is another great time to build the bond and recognize employees. If you make recognition a daily feature, it will work better for you and your employees.

Remember that this thing we call engagement is a process—day by day.

You're Too Busy?

You're the general manger of a large hotel, and you don't have time to work with your staff as I described—or do you? I would challenge you to start slowly, not every day, but a couple of days a week. If you're still shaking your head and thinking that it is impossible, let me help.

Mr. Marriott visited and inspected every one of his establishments four times a year, even after his company grew to hundreds of restaurants and hotels. Now, are you really too busy?

If you really want to make an impression, show up on Saturday morning and help out. I am guessing that you probably don't work a lot of Saturdays. Show up on a weekend morning, a day you typically would not be seen at the hotel, ready to work with your employees and you will impress them. Just be prepared for a lot of questions, especially this one: What are you doing here?

7 FAIRNESS

This is another topic that surprised me; you would think that with all the legal action taking place in the United States, people would be minding their Ps and Qs. Apparently not; but possibly not so apparent are some of the things that employees consider fair.

I think the number one fairness claim is scheduling. According to employees, the schedules may not be fair in many ways; the most common complaint is the timeliness of the new schedule. This provides a huge opportunity to help with the engagement of your entire staff; just make the schedule and post it on time.

 Here is the issue: You are busy, so you wait until the last minute to post a schedule. That simple action in one swift stroke shows all of your employees that you could not care less about their time away from work. Think about that just a bit. It takes about 20 to 30 minutes to make a work schedule for fewer than 50 employees, something that you could knock out on Monday morning and post in a timely way, so that everyone could make plans weeks in advance. It is a simple solution to one of the top complaints from employees.

Can I Please Have a Day Off?

The other issue employees have with scheduling is, of course, days off. Most want weekends off but don't get them. It may often appear that an individual or group of individuals frequently gets weekends off. Here is a very simple solution to that huge issue: Rotate the weekends off and never tell people when hiring them that they will get weekends off.

With the issues of scheduling and weekends dealt with, let me deal with the F word: favoritism. It is very hard to not show favoritism to your top performers, your A team, the ones who have your back, but it is not impossible. If you want a team of high performers, then you have to treat them all the same, as high performers. When you show favoritism, you are building walls between you and the other members of the team, in some cases even the person you favor. It can be awkward or even embarrassing for them.

As I have mentioned, avoiding the show of favoritism is not easy, but it can be done. Favoritism is a disease that will suck the life out of your team, because if you are favoring someone, the rest of the team is lacking communication, training, respect, recognition and fairness. Take a little time to correct this issue and you will save yourself many headaches and lots of time. Start being aware of your behavior around all associates, make sure you give equal amounts of time and resources to each and every one of them.

I'll Be Right With You

Another issue that falls under the banner of unfairness is understaffing. I understand the financial constraints of running a business all too well. However, those of us in operations tend to lean too much on what is easy, cutting the middle instead of adding to the top. What is the first thing that came to your mind when you read "adding to the top"? I am pretty sure it was sales, and when you think about sales, what is the first thing that comes to your mind? Sales calls? Oh, the dreaded sales call! But wait a minute. Isn't that what we have sales managers and sales departments for? Just about any sales professional will tell you that 80% of your sales come from 20% of your customers. So you had better take good care of your 20% or their numbers will dwindle.

When you run understaffed, you are not taking care of your customers. You are reducing your payroll and affiliated expenses; you are not being more efficient. You are asking your employees to do two or three times the work they did several years ago and not compensating them accordingly, so they see that as unfair.

So let's bring it home. You are the general manager of a hotel, and you are asked to oversee your current hotel and two other hotels with no extra compensation for your increased responsibilities. That would be insane, right? That is what a lot of you are asking your hourly employees to do. You have done a great job cutting your expenses, but at the same time you are disengaging your workforce. What effect do you think it is having on your customers? More than you realize or want to believe.

> When you run understaffed, you are not taking care of your customers.

You see, your consumers/customers/guests like to feel important when they are spending money with you. When you make them wait because there are not enough employees to deliver the service they want, you are not making them feel important. This goes beyond waiting in line or being inconvenienced.

The Pool Stinks

When staying in a hotel, the number one must-have for travelers is cleanliness. This really should go without saying. But when you are understaffed and ask housekeepers to clean more rooms, the level of the cleanliness goes down. It does not take a rocket scientist to figure out that if a housekeeper can clean a room thoroughly in 30 minutes and you nevertheless give that housekeeper only 25 minutes, something is not getting done. That might be acceptable for a short period of time, but over the course of a month, you will have a hotel full of dirty rooms; and what about the maintenance of the rooms and the facility as a whole?

Nothing is more annoying than checking into a hotel for which I just paid north of $150 per night and finding that the TV is not working properly, the HVAC is not cooling the room properly and the pool smells funny. Don't laugh, I checked into a hotel a few years ago with my family (wife and three kids) and when we got to the pool, it not only smelled funny, there was stuff floating in the water. That happens when you don't have enough employees working to maintain your property.

My wife and I went away for a romantic weekend several years ago to a little inn on the Outer Banks of North Carolina. I had done plenty of research and found the perfect spot. A couple of the amenities that this particular property promoted were in-room Jacuzzi tubs, gourmet continental breakfast and a private swimming pool. We were both excited to get there and check out this wonderful little inn. We pulled up, and the curbside appeal was good. We checked in with no issue; our room was a bit small, but it had a large king-size bed and,—don't forget—a Jacuzzi tub. After hauling all of our luggage to the room, I did an inspection. I won't list all of the cleanliness issues I found, but the room was not good.

Since it was a bit late, I told my wife to fire up the Jacuzzi while I went to get some ice (no refrigerator in the room). The ice machine was on the other side of the building, and upon my return I heard this awful noise. It sounded like a wood chipper running. It was 11 p.m., so I was sure the grounds crew was not working on the landscaping. As I returned, became convinced that the noise was coming from our room. When I opened the door my wife was laughing so hard she could not speak; the noise was coming from the Jacuzzi. I turned it off and we decided we would go take a late dip in the pool. As we approached it, I noticed something floating in the middle, an extraordinarily large piece of tree bark. Apparently earlier that day, a tree had fallen and the staff had neglected to clean the pool.

I could go on about how many things were wrong, like the continental breakfast that was far from being a gourmet's meal. The morning we checked out, I asked a few questions and let the manager know that the Jacuzzi could use some maintenance, and I found out that the inn was understaffed. The manager he gave me several reasons, none of which I cared about.

I just touched on a couple of very prevalent issues, but there are many more and they all lead to one thing: customers who are not satisfied. You are saving a few dollars to make your profit and loss statement look good, but your customers are going to find other hotels and tell all their friends. I would encourage you to rethink the understaffing strategy; it is not fair to your employees or to your customers. It is also costing you money in the long run.

So we have covered the top five reasons for employees being disengaged, and all of them seem rather simple to fix, don't they? That is because they *are* simple to fix, but remember that sometimes simple is not easy. It will take a shift in your thought process to make these behaviors part of your daily routine, but I know you can do it. Just make the commitment to yourself and get started today. Remember that it is a process, and that things are not going to become perfect in a day. It will take some time. How long? That will depend on the current level of engagement at your organization.

If it is pretty low, it took a while to drop down there, so it will take a while to get it where it needs to be.

8 VICE PRESIDENT OF ENGAGEMENT

Does your organization have a vice president of engagement? You have a vice president of sales, a vice president of operations, a vice president of food and beverage, a vice president of finance; you have managers who are focused on managing revenue, etc. You probably have a vice president of human resources, and engagement really does seem to fall under this umbrella of responsibility. But in many cases, human resources personnel simply are not equipped to handle the day-to-day process of engagement.

There needs to be a leader in the organization who is responsible for growing s engagement, just as other leaders are responsible for growing their own disciplines. Back in the mid-1980s, when yield management, now called revenue management, started to become popular, companies began making it a daily process. Now we have revenue managers, mainly because operations managers could not give revenue the attention it needed or deserved. Because engagement is also a daily process, don't you think you would have a much better chance of leveraging this powerful process if you had someone to manage it on a daily basis?

Engagement, as I have often said, is not a human resources initiative that managers are reminded of once a year when doing a survey. It is a key strategic initiative that drives employee performance, accomplishment and improvement every day. It is the outcome of your organization's interaction with its employees.

9 CHANGES EFFECTING ENGAGEMENT

When I started working in hotels, it was obvious that the hourly employee was valued, and management spent time getting to know and nurture employees, developing them into managers and into more productive employees. The communication coming from the leadership was excellent. My supervisors communicated key information that helped me become a company man. They let me know why we did what we did; they taught me the values and the mission of the company. They did not just read this out of an orientation manual; they talked about the goals and the mission every day. They demonstrated the type of commitment they wanted from all employees by doing the work themselves.

In other words, they embraced the values and believed in them, and they expected employees to do the same.

Hey, They Already Know What to Do

Think about the value that is gained by running your operation in a manner that develops and builds your company's strengths. You build a pool of potential managers, you build a pool of excellent employees; when you do so, your employees are happy, they are very enthusiastic, and they have a good feeling about the company. This enthusiasm spills over to the guest/customer. Employees understand that the guest/customer is the reason they have work to do. Thus their mission is to serve the guest/customer.

How could an environment like this go wrong? How could such a process crumble and start to go in the opposite direction? It happened gradually. The manager who spent most of his or her time with employees and guests was effective and thus was given more responsibility, which started to eat into the time spent with the employees and guests. These managers were told that they needed to become more like business owners and be responsible for their business, which meant watching the numbers.

Managers became more and more involved with profitability and were being held more accountable for it, which took more time from employees and guests. Managers started spending more time in their offices reviewing sales reports; managing revenue; learning about market penetration, payroll, healthcare and many other new responsibilities. Gradually the time they once spent with employees and guests fell to only minutes a day. Now there are some managers who rarely see guests, let alone carry on conversations with them. They see employees, but not as frequently or as meaningfully as they had in the past.

I have read many employee comments indicating that senior managers at their hotels do not even acknowledge workers as they pass in hallways. Many of the comments indicate that managers sometimes do not even know who their employees are. This is absurd.

This change in management style is the main reason for the lack of engagement in most organizations. It got so bad at one point that management companies started mandating that general managers spend some time in the morning shaking hands in the lobby. This is usually referred to as being a lobby lizard and can be a very successful approach if used consistently.

This business-oriented approach can apply not only to the hospitality industry but also to 80% of the workers in the United States. But because this change erosion of engagement didn't happen quickly, it was not fully understood or recognized. It was a shift in culture, a shift from taking care of the employees to taking care of the business.

Mountain Climbing

I remember attending a national general manager conference for one of my employers during this time of change. Jim Hayhurst Sr. had been hired to speak at the conference. Hayhurst, a motivational speaker, had climbed Mount Everest in 1988, and he related the obstacles and challenges of that climb to bringing about change in business. If I remember correctly, he threw in some information about leadership responsibility and the team-building thought processes, but the key to his message was a question: Are you on the right mountain? After he spoke, one of the leaders in the organization took the stage and broke it down for us, explaining how he wanted us to receive that message. Basically it was this: If your personal values don't match up with ours, you are on the wrong mountain, meaning that if you don't like the way we are doing things, go somewhere else, because we are not going to change.

This was the beginning of what I call the accountability phase of the change in management style. General Managers had to run their businesses from a different place; they had to manage from their offices instead of managing by walking around.

Are you on the right mountain?

The new style required much attention to profit and loss statements, revenue management, sales funnels and the administrative side of the business. I believe there are many businesses that can be run effectively with that approach, but not in an industry that is labor-intensive. If you have no or few employees, it may be acceptable to live in spreadsheets, but ignoring your staff is certain to cost you more than you think.

Those of us who are in the business of helping organizations create and grow engagement have seen some rather significant changes over the last couple of decades as well. I remember the first time I sat down in the grand ballroom of the hotel to take an employee opinion survey. I thought it was pretty cool that the people who ran this huge company even cared what I would mark on the questionnaire—and I remember they *did* care. I also remember the first time I received the results of such a survey as a general manager and finding areas to celebrate and areas that needed attention. I thought the process was awesome and a very helpful experience for everyone involved. Today surveys are often done on smartphones and laptops, and very few companies use paper surveys. This means progress. With the aid of computers and the Internet, we can receive data and create reports in the bat of an eye. Unfortunately, along with this progress came some changes that are actually hurting the engagement movement in some ways.

$E = MC^2$

It appears that scientists and psychologists have taken control of the survey process. I am sure there is some benefit to this, but the negative outweighs it in many instances. The survey was created to give an organization a snapshot of its engagement situation. The survey tells managers which practices they can celebrate and continue and which practices they need to change. This means that communication with the client about the data collected in surveys needs to be simple and easy to understand and must be presented in a way that will allow the client to take action. Simplicity is not often in evidence, however. With thousands of data points and multiple ways to view data, clients can be overwhelmed. These clients will experience paralysis by analysis. You should not need a PhD to understand engagement.

> "They are under my desk. I use them for a footstool."

Such paralyzed clients will do nothing with the results. I recall meeting with a potential client and trying to determine what method her company used to create action plans as well as to monitor the implementation and progress of those plans, so I asked her what she did with the results. She misunderstood my question and thought I was asking what she did with the reports. She said, "They are under my desk, I use them for a footstool." The reports were so overwhelming and difficult to understand that they were not used at all.

I imagine that if the scientists and psychologists who designed the surveys were the ones using the data, everything would be fine, but in most cases the people in charge of interpreting and analyzing the results are human resources managers and operational managers. Believe me, they do not have time to sit down for hours trying to get a handle on engagement; they need a process that is easy to use and quick, one that they can scan

> You should not need a PhD. to understand engagement.

to find the areas that need immediate attention. There is a place for the science and psychology of surveys,

but that place is not in the communication the end
users.

10 WHERE IT ALL BEGINS

I am pretty sure you know where it all begins—at the top. Just look at the peak of the pyramid on your organizational chart. This is where it begins. If your organization lacks engagement, the process of developing it must start at the top; your organizational leader is the one who must start it.

This means that the leader of the organization must understand engagement and its benefits. The leader must make engagement a key element in the culture of the organization and communicate that priority to employees. When he or she does so, engagement flows slowly down the organizational chart to the hourly employees.

Managers are Employees

Another factor to keep in mind as you prepare to make a culture shift or enhancement: Managers are employees too. The fact that they are paid salaries does not exclude them from engagement; they need to be engaged as well. In fact, the more engaged the managers are, the more likely they will produce teams of engaged hourly employees.

I have read many survey comments indicating that management does not follow the rules and that management says one thing and does another. Your management team needs to be communicating your mission, your goals and your values. If management deeds don't match management communication, you have a problem. When your management team is engaged, this is usually not an issue.

It seems to me that in most organizations good managers are scarce. I believe the number one reason for poor management is, as I have mentioned before, that they are promoted to higher positions because they were good at their jobs but then did not receive proper managerial training. Being good at a job does not mean being good at managing other people who do the same job. The skills needed to be a good manager are vastly different from the skills needed to be an accountant, front desk clerk or server in a restaurant. So in many cases, when good employees are promoted to management posts without specific training, the general manager is doing a terrible disservice to the employee by promoting him or her to management.

The skill set successful managers need is diverse; they need to be able to give direction and constructive criticism, set goals, build relationships, hold people accountable, delegate, remain involved but not so close as to micromanage, etc.

Very rarely will an organization have the ability to train a new manager in all of these areas; in fact the lack of training for new management skills is amazing. In most cases, the training revolves around standard operating procedures, the policies and the tangible tasks for which a new manager will be responsible. Other needed skills include relationship-building, verbal communication, written communication and negotiation.

I also believe that many companies have a misconception of what contributes to good management and therefore have difficulty spotting a bad manager. And when they do spot a bad manager, their inability to terminate him or her is borderline ridiculous.

I understand that in today's society, most companies fear legal issues, but trust me when I say that a bad manager will cost you more money over the long haul than a wrongful termination suit. In some cases, a bad manager is good at some aspects of his or her job, and the company may focus on that while being blind to the fact that such managers may create more issues than they resolve. Of course there are also managers who stay in their jobs because of their ability to make friends with their bosses. Don't get caught in that trap; it will come back to bite you later. There is nothing wrong with having friendly relationships with your subordinate managers, but don't let them take advantage of those relationships.

Expectations

The engagement process is driven from the top down, as are all important initiatives. Do not expect your hourly employees to be engaged if their supervisors are not. Do not expect your supervisors to be engaged if their managers are not. Do not expect your managers to be engaged if their upper level managers are not. Can you see where this is going? Straight to the top!

It takes considerable courage to stand up and be the leader, but no one will follow you if you do not lead for the right reasons. People want to be inspired, they want to feel fulfilled and they need to connect with their leaders.

Great leaders all have one thing in common: They serve their people. They remove obstacles and excuses and lead by example. They have the true spirit of service. The best of them manage by walking around. They get down in the trenches and shake hands with their people, they work beside their people and, most important, they have conversations with their people. They listen, they remove obstacles, they reject excuses and they inspire others in these conversations. They connect on a personal level, not in a group. They look into the eyes of their employees and learn from them as well as leading them.

Great leaders are always asking questions and trying to learn more from their people; they never seem to be satisfied with the way things are because they want them to be better. They also expect this from their employees. The best leaders look for the good in all people, and they also tend to coax the good out of others. Everybody makes a mistake now and then, but good leaders don't focus on those mistakes; they focus on what has been done correctly and they give recognition and praise for good work because they know this will inspire employees to continue to excel. You see, all people want to feel important.

Great leaders recognize this and try to help others feel important. Building a culture of engagement will not be a lengthy process for a good leader.

11 REASONS

Amazing numbers of studies have been done on engagement as well as statistics; they all indicate that engagement should be a very important focus of any organization run by people with the desire to grow and prosper. There are two statistics that should convince the leaders of any organization to take heed:

- A Gallup poll indicates that organizations with high degrees of engagement outperform others by more than 202%.
- Another Gallup poll indicates that only 13% of employees worldwide are engaged at work.

For those of you who have thought that there was no way for you to promote engagement in your company because doing so would cost money and change many of the ways you do business, I would say this: Engagement is not free. It will take an investment in time and money. If you choose not to invest in a culture of engagement within your organization, you will continue to spend the money in other ways, for frequent recruitment and training and in lost productivity as well as lost customers/guests.

You have the basics, which are all you need to build an organization of engagement. Now it is now up to you. I would suggest starting immediately and slowly. Don't become overwhelmed with change. Embrace it and move forward.

I certainly hope you will choose rjs data group to assist with your engagement survey, but the important thing is to do one, no matter who helps. You need to know where you are and what your issues are so you can start growing engagement.

There are many things to consider when you are conducting an engagement survey, whether you are starting your first one, or have decided that your current survey needs some tweaks.

Ask the Right Questions

One of the vital keys to receiving data that will help you grow your engagement is asking the right questions. Because the questionnaire should be built around your company's culture, mission and beliefs, there is no standard set of questions. If you are told there is such a standard, run as fast as you can.

We expect and want excellence from our employees, so don't ask mediocre questions. Instead of asking if employees like coming to work most of the time, ask them if they are excited to come to work every day. Don't ask them if they believe the communication they receive is adequate; ask them if the communication they receive is the best.

I will say this; there are some questions that are asked by many companies. For example, most ask some sort of overall question to gauge how employees feel when they consider the entire experience at work. A lot of companies ask about tools and supplies to determine if their employees agree that they have everything they need to succeed in their jobs. Answers to such questions are wanted by most companies, and although they may help with operational issues, they do not determine your engagement level. There are some questions that have often been asked in surveys that I would steer you away from; most are questions about compensation.

Compensation questions typically should not be asked because companies often cannot act on the answers. Remember that when you ask an employee a question in a formal setting like an engagement survey, it implies that you are willing to do something to correct the issue if necessary. And compensation questions are always the lowest- scoring questions on surveys.

I can remember when companies that got negative answers to compensation questions turned next to wage surveys of their areas. This was really just adding salt to the open wound. Employees want to make more money and have better benefits, regardless of their positions.

Wouldn't you like to make more money for all the hard work you do for your company? Of course you would; you are dedicated and give a large portion of your life to this organization, and you deserve more money. You know your employees want more money, so why ask a question when you know the answer will remind them of a perceived negative?

> Wouldn't you like to make more money for all the hard work you do for your company?

Of course, there are certain circumstances that could make a compensation question legitimate. One example: If the company just switched to a new insurance carrier, you will want to find out if the new insurance company is treating your employees as promised in terms of coverage and cost. You could ask that question immediately after the switch, but you would not want to continue asking it on later surveys.

When you are developing your questions, it is a good idea to consult with your vendor, which should have enough experience to know the pitfalls and proper approaches.

Promote | Promote | Promote

Marketing the survey to employees is also a vital piece of the process. You want to start talking about the survey at least two weeks before the start date. You should discuss the process in all meetings and daily huddles. You want to make sure everyone is aware of the survey and uncover any concerns that employees may have. Confidentiality is very important, and employees should know that their responses to questions will never be known by their immediate supervisors, managers or corporate officers.

Any significant change in the behavior of managers in the couple of weeks before an engagement survey is going to be detected by your employees. They will know what you are up to, so don't even try it. We get so many comments about managers who act as though they are respectful for a couple of weeks before the survey and who return to their normal behavior immediately after the survey. Managers don't need to buy pizza for everyone to increase their scores. They would be better off spending all that time and energy on becoming better managers; then they would not have to worry about survey results.

I guess it is human nature to try to determine who said something negative. Managers can take things personally, become defensive and try to determine who said what about them. This is obviously the complete opposite of what they should be doing, and you should beware of the detective manager. At the same time, employees should be aware that when they enter comments into a survey, the way they express their opinions may affect their anonymity. If they typically use certain phrases in normal speech, they should avoid using them in written comments. The more information like this that employees receive upfront about completing surveys, the more comfortable they become with the process and the more honest the answers will be. If possible, employees should be given the opportunity to take the survey away from the workplace.

No longer should we herd employees into a large meeting room and bribe them with cookies and soda in order to conduct a survey. We should simply give them what they need to access the survey and let them respond. They should be able to take the survey on their smart phones, tablets, netbooks, laptops, etc. If you think your workforce is not computer-literate, think again. Better yet, get out of your office and go eat lunch with your employees and watch them text their children and friends while they eat. Wake up. If you think this way, you are underestimating your staff. In a very large organization, there may be one or two people who don't know how to point and click, but they will know someone who can assist them.

So you start marketing or promoting the survey a couple of weeks before it happens; you have informed everyone, overcome their concerns, and you are ready to start. Don't stop your promotion until the last day of the survey, because participation is another key to a successful survey. If you did not promote the survey, the only people who would complete it would be the ones that are upset about something, so your results would be skewed to the negative. You want to shoot for 100% participation so you hear from everyone. If you have already started managing by walking around, you will have no issues with promoting the survey, and your level of participation will be great.

It is also important that you partner with a vendor who can quickly turn your results around. I can remember surveys from years ago, when we had to wait three or four weeks for results. This is just totally unacceptable, regardless of the size of the survey. We turn most of our surveys around in three days, maximum..

When the results are back, what do you do with them? What have you done with them in the past? I mentioned previously that you need to beware of the detective manager; don't be that manager. Understand that you are human; you make mistakes and you are not perfect in all areas of your life. Use this knowledge as a tool to help you grow engagement levels at your company. You need to digest the information and understand the reports, and your vendor/partner should be able to supply you with reports that are easy to understand. Believe me when I tell you that a lot of vendors will try to impress clients with their thousands of data points and graphs that are virtually impossible to understand.

Discovery Meeting

Once you have a firm grasp of the results, it is time to conduct a discovery meeting. The way this meeting is conducted depends on the size of your organization. If you have a large full-service hotel, for instance, you will conduct several of these meetings in various departments. If your hotel is a smaller select- service property, you will conduct one all-employee meeting.

Discovery meetings can be extremely advantageous or total flops. The key to success in such meetings is atmosphere. This meeting is not for the management to point fingers and be defensive, as a detective manager might be. The key to discovery meetings is to move forward and make the correct changes or tweaks to grow engagement. An engagement survey is not worth the broadband it requires if you do not act on the results. I used to say it was not worth the paper it was printed on but hey, this is the new millennium.

How do you set the right tone or atmosphere in a discovery meeting? You have to speak from your heart; you need to convey to your employees that you are excited about some of the results and may need some help understanding others. In the meeting, you will disclose the results.

I believe you should review every question in the survey because your employees will consider some questions to be more important than others, and you don't want to make anyone feel left out of the meeting. Discuss the areas in which you are doing well. Celebrate and give some recognition to employees who help the hotel achieve that success. Explain to your employees that you want to make the company a better place to work and that the process of doing so will take some time. Pay special attention to three to five survey questions that scored the worst and assure your employees that these are the areas on which you want the greatest focus. Ask your employees for suggestions about how you as the leader can make effective changes in these areas. In essence, you are asking your employees to write your action plans.

If you do this successfully, they will take ownership of the plans and help make sure that they are implemented. They will also help with follow up.

Goal Setting

The goals you set for change should be aggressive but obtainable, and you should identify expectations so everyone knows the plan and works to help it succeed. You will have stragglers who either do not want to grow or do not buy in to the engagement process. This is typical, and you need to spend some time with these employees to help them overcome their resistance. You need to show them why their help and support will benefit them as well as the entire team.

How are your Action Plans working? I hope that after the survey is done and the plans are implemented, you and your managers can keep a moving in the right direction. This is one of the reasons why a semiannual survey is most beneficial. Every six months you will have the opportunity to check the progress of your action plans. This also keeps everyone involved and thinking about engagement.

This is where I should point out that you need to watch the good survey numbers as well. Make sure you are not slipping in areas in which you were once outstanding. Unfortunately, good numbers sometimes hurt us more than they help. For instance, if you look only at what you are doing well, you are missing the areas that need improvement. You can't just look at survey results as a whole; you need to look at them question by question. A negative response may be hidden among positive responses. I know everyone wants to see the overall score, but don't let a good overall score hurt you.

Now it is up to you.

If you have questions about the engagement process or about creating and taking a survey, please don't hesitate to send me an email. I would love to help and look forward to the opportunity.

ABOUT THE AUTHOR

Randy Starr has worked in the hospitality industry for more than 25 years. He started as a part-time front desk clerk after his original interview for a housekeeping position was rejected. He worked in all departments of hotels and earned his first management position in a few short years.

His passion for his family has always kept him grounded and was eventually the reason why he left corporate America to start his own business, rjs data group.

His dedication to helping organizations find an effective engagement culture is second to none.

rjs data group is an engagement survey company with cutting-edge technology that clients can easily understand.

 Randy Starr is available for consultation and speaking engagements. Contact him at www.rjsdatagroup.com or on LinkedIn.